## PAMELA DENISE BROWN
Smart Book For Kids
In 5 Languages

# Sit In Your Seat

526 TO 530 OF 700
Educational Books
5 Books In 1 In 5 Languages
English, Spanish, Swahili, French & Italian

# ACKNOWLEDGEMENT

I Would Like To Acknowledge The
CREATOR OF HEAVEN AND EARTH (GOD)
FOR ALL THAT HE HAS Given Me.
Thanking God I Am For My Talents and
Gifts.
I Recognize That The Lord Gave Me This
Gift, Which Allows Me To Share With
Children And Everyone That Participates In
The Reading Of The Literary Material That
I Produce Through The Commission Of God.

## Thank You Lord God

I Will Forever Be Grateful
For Your Trust In Me

# WORDS
# ARE
# POWERFUL

Pamela Denise Brown
Goodwill Ambassador
For The Positive Cultivation Of Children

My EDUCATIONAL Collection Of Books
Are For The Advancement Of Children.
I'm Not Selling Books, I Am However,
Providing Thought Leading Reinforcements,
That Can Be Simplistically Utilized As
Reference Material, As An Investment In
The Positive Cultivation Of Children's Lives.

A little information about the author, My Educational Books are designed to educate children, to transform the way a child thinks, to better children so they can become successful people. I write educational books to help children develop and grow psychologically.

As an Ambassador for the cultivation of children, I am a trusted source moving to inspire children with innovative ideas, creating evolutionary advancements by urging children to be open to new ways of thinking.

I present children with an opportunity to replicate and scale the ideas from the pages of the educational literature I produce into sustainable change, by shaping the lives of children from any background, community, age, ethnicity or gender. My goal is to give children balance and broaden their understanding as it relates to "co-existing" in society as a coherent whole.

I have codified what I know and placed it within reach. I am strategically reaching into the mind of every child that reads the literary information that I have produced in my Collection of Educational Books.

Copyright © 2016 Pamela Denise Brown.
All rights reserved. No part of this book may be
used or reproduced by any means, graphic,
electronic, or mechanical, including photocopying,
recording, taping or by any information storage
retrieval system without the written permission of
the publishers except in the case of brief
quotations embodied in critical articles and
reviews.

Books Speak For You books may be ordered
through booksellers or by contacting:
Booksspeakforyou.com
The views expressed in this work are solely those
of the author.
Any illustration provided by iStock and such images
are being used for illustrative purposes.
Certain stock imagery © iStock.
ISBN: 978-1-64050-161-4
Library of Congress Control Number: 2017906406

# THE BOOKS

700 BOOKS IN 60 DAYS
I was commissioned by God to first write 40 Books in 40 days, then 100 books in 100 days on October 1, 2015, which I completed on January 8, 2016, commissioned again June 7, 2016 to write 700 books in 60 days starting July, 2016.

# INTRODUCTION

My Collection Of EDUCATIONAL Books are designed to foster the social development of children psychologically. My books are designed to teach children values, morals and reintroduce manners to them. I believe the books I write will transform the minds of children from any community, background, race ethnicity and age, which ultimately will cause them to pause, to think and make better choices.

My EDUCATIONAL Books are designed to effectuate change and influence success in the lives of every child.

The EDUCATIONAL Books in the Collection are Reinforcements to Learning.

My EDUCATIONAL books will help build children's self-esteem and confidence to a level that will help them socially engage in a diverse world with confidence and harmony and ultimately prepare them for life.

Children Stand silently trying to open a door that cannot be opened with hands...
Written 11/23/2015 11:18 a.m.

If to educate is your objective than to learn is your AIM...
Written 11/21/2015 1:41 a.m.

With Even Strokes Caress The Mind,
With Gentle Words Handle A Child,
With Excitement Finish The Race,
With Commitment Help A Child
Stay In Place.
LOVE IS EVERLASTING WITH GOD.
Written: July 3, 2016 @ 10:06 pm.

If you really want to enhance the life of a child, your first step is to see yourself like a child and then approach the child like you see yourself.
Written: 11/21/2015  2:22 a.m.

If You're In A "CROWDED" Room and A Child Is Sitting "ALONE" That Can Only Mean The Room Is EMPTY.....
Written 11/21/2015 1:42 a.m.

# Sit In Your Seat

# English

# 526

The alarms at Pamela's Elementary School were ringing uncontrollably. No one knew whether it was a false alarm or an actually threat.

Sit In Your Seat, Ms. Jackson kindly asked the students so she could listen to see if there would be an announcement over the loud speaker.

Hurry Up class,
hurry
 Ms. Jackson asked again.

Sit In Your Seat, until I find out what
is going on.

The students were puzzled,
running for their seats at the same
time, with one exception,
Tony.

Tony was a student Ms. Jackson loved, but Tony had focusing problems, which often forced Ms. Jackson to stop and redirect him in the class.

Yes, Ms. Jackson,

Tony replied.

The children were talking loud amongst themselves, wondering why the alarm was going off.

Silence,
be silent for a minute students, Ms.
Jackson asked politely.

I need to hear the announcement.

Then it came,

The

# announcement.

The principal got on the loud speaker
and announced the school
superintendent's arrival.

The principal wanted to inform the teachers that the superintendent was touring the school to see what all the bragging was about.

It was said that Pamela's' Elementary School students scored the highest in reading and math in the country and they were also ranked most polite and organized.

After the announcement, everyone was relieved.

The students started getting out of their seats, running to the door to see if the superintendent was coming to their class.

Sit In Your Seat, Ms. Jackson said to her class.

As soon as the students sat in their seats, in walked the superintendent.

# WOW,

what a well behaved class.

Look at this, everybody's in their SEAT!

NOW GUYS, do you see the importance of sitting in your seat, Ms. Jackson asked.

The Superintendent congratulated the class on their success and left to continue the tour of the school.

Students, in the space below in your own words, write why you think it's important to remain in your seat while you're in class.

_____

_____

_____

_____

_____

_____

_____

_____

_____

_____

_____

_____

_____

_____

_____

_____

_____

_____

Do you believe following instructions in class is important for your academic development?

_____

_____

_____

_____

_____

_____

_____

_____

_____

_____

_____

_____

_____

_____

_____

_____

_____

_____

Why do you believe the teachers want students to remain in their seats while teaching?

_____

_____

_____

_____

_____

_____

_____

_____

_____

_____

_____

_____

_____

_____

_____

_____

_____

_____

Do you believe you learn more when everyone in the class is following the rules of the classroom?

_____

_____

_____

_____

_____

_____

_____

_____

_____

_____

_____

_____

_____

_____

_____

_____

_____

_____

Do you believe rules are important in a classroom or do you believe you should be allowed to do whatever you want?.

_____

_____

_____

_____

_____

_____

_____

_____

_____

_____

_____

_____

_____

_____

_____

_____

_____

_____

_____

_____

Do you believe sitting in your seat keeps you safe and accountable?  Explain your thoughts.

_____

_____

_____

_____

_____

_____

_____

_____

_____

_____

_____

_____

_____

_____

_____

_____

_____

_____

Do you believe the teacher controls the classroom better when everyone is in their seat?.

_____

_____

_____

_____

_____

_____

_____

_____

_____

_____

_____

_____

_____

_____

_____

_____

_____

_____

# Sit In Your Seat Spanish 527

Las alarmas de la Escuela Primaria de Pamela resonaban incontrolablemente. Nadie sabía si era una falsa alarma o una amenaza real.

Sit en tu asiento, la Sra. Jackson amablemente preguntó a los estudiantes para que ella pudiera escuchar para ver si habría un anuncio sobre el altoparlante.

Hurry Up clase, prisa
La Sra. Jackson preguntó de nuevo.
Siéntate en tu asiento, hasta que descubra
lo que está pasando.


Los estudiantes estaban desconcertados,
Corriendo por sus asientos al mismo tiempo,
con una excepción,
Tony.

Tony era una estudiante a la que amaba
Jackson, pero Tony tenía problemas de
enfoque, lo que a menudo obligaba a la Sra.
Jackson a detenerlo y redirigirlo en la
clase.


Sí, Sra. Jackson,
Tony respondió.
Los niños estaban hablando fuerte entre sí,
preguntándose por qué la alarma se estaba
apagando.

Silencio, callen por un minuto a los
estudiantes, la Sra. Jackson preguntó
cortésmente.
Necesito oír el anuncio.


Entonces vino,
El anuncio.


El director tomó el altavoz y anunció la
llegada del superintendente de la escuela.


El director quería informar a los maestros
que el superintendente estaba de gira por la
escuela para ver de qué se trataba todo el
jactarse.


Se dijo que los estudiantes de Primaria de
Pamela obtuvieron el puntaje más alto en
lectura y matemáticas en el país y también
fueron clasificados como los más educados
y organizados.

Después del anuncio, todos quedaron aliviados. Los estudiantes comenzaron a salir de sus asientos, corriendo a la puerta para ver si el superintendente venía a su clase.

Sit en tu asiento, la Sra. Jackson dijo a su clase.

Tan pronto como los estudiantes se sentaron en sus asientos, en caminó el superintendente.

WOW,
Qué clase bien educada.

Mira esto, todos están en su asiento!


NOW GUYS, ¿ve usted la importancia de sentarse en su asiento, la Sra. Jackson preguntó.

# Sit In Your Seat Swahili 528

The kengele katika Pamela Elementary School walikuwa kupigia uncontrollably. Hakuna mtu alijua iwapo ilikuwa kengele ya uongo kweli tishio.

Sit Katika Seat yako, Bi Jackson kindly aliuliza wanafunzi ili aweze kusikiliza ili kuona kama kutakuwa na tangazo juu ya msemaji kubwa.

Hurry Up darasani, haraka
 Bi Jackson aliuliza tena.
Kukaa Katika Seat yako, hata mimi kujua
nini kinachoendelea.

The wanafunzi walikuwa puzzled,
mbio kwa viti vyao wakati huo huo, isipokuwa
moja,
Tony.

Tony alikuwa mwanafunzi Bi Jackson
kupendwa, lakini Tony alikuwa kulenga
matatizo, ambayo mara nyingi kulazimishwa
Bi Jackson kuacha na kuelekeza kwake
darasani.

Yes, Bi Jackson,
Tony alijibu.
watoto walikuwa kuzungumza kubwa
miongoni mwao wenyewe, anashangaa kwa
nini alarm alikuwa anaenda mbali.

Silence, kuwa kimya kwa wanafunzi dakika,
Bi Jackson aliuliza kwa upole.
Nahitaji kusikia tangazo.

Then ikaenda,
tangazo.

mkuu got juu ya msemaji kubwa na alitangaza kuwasili shule ya kamanda.

The mkuu alitaka kuwajulisha walimu kwamba msimamizi alikuwa katika ziara ya shule na kuona nini majisifu zote ilikuwa juu.

It ilikuwa alisema kuwa Pamela 'Elementary School wanafunzi alifunga juu katika kusoma na math nchini na pia walikuwa nafasi kama wengi heshima na kupangwa.

After tangazo hilo, kila mtu alikuwa kuondoka. wanafunzi kuanza kupata nje ya viti vyao, kukimbia kwa mlango ili kuona kama msimamizi alikuwa anakuja darasa lao.

Sit Katika Seat yako, Bi Jackson alisema darasani kwake.

Haraka kama wanafunzi ameketi katika viti vyao, katika kutembea msimamizi.

WOW,
kile darasa vizuri tulipokuwa.

Angalia hii, kila mtu ni katika SEAT zao!

NOW GUYS, unaona umuhimu wa kukaa katika kiti yako, Bi Jackson aliuliza.

Superintendent aliwapongeza darasa juu ya mafanikio yao na kushoto kuendelea ziara la shule.

# Sit In Your Seat French 529

Les alarmes de l'école primaire de Pamela sonnaient incontrôlables. Personne

ne savait si c'était une fausse alerte une menace réelle.

Sit à votre place, Mme Jackson a aimablement demandé aux élèves afin qu'elle puisse écouter pour voir s'il y aurait une annonce au-dessus du haut-parleur.

Le cours de la classe, dépêchez-vous
 Mlle Jackson a demandé à nouveau.
Asseyez-vous à votre place, jusqu'à ce que
je découvre ce qui se passe.

Les étudiants étaient perplexes,
Courent pour leurs sièges en même temps, à
une exception près,
Tony.

Tony était une étudiante que Mme Jackson
aimait, mais Tony avait des problèmes de
concentration, ce qui obligeait souvent Mme
Jackson à s'arrêter et à le rediriger dans la
classe.


Oui, madame Jackson,
Répondit Tony.
Les enfants parlaient fort entre eux, se
demandant pourquoi l'alarme allait.

Silence, taisez-vous pour quelques minutes,
a demandé Mme Jackson poliment.

J'ai besoin d'entendre l'annonce.

Alors il arriva,
L'annonce.


La directrice de l'école est arrivée sur le haut-parleur et a annoncé l'arrivée du surintendant scolaire.


Le directeur voulait informer les enseignants que le surintendant faisait le tour de l'école pour voir de quoi il s'agissait.


On a dit que les élèves de l'école élémentaire de Pamela avaient obtenu les meilleurs résultats en lecture et en mathématiques au pays et ils étaient également classés comme les plus polis et les plus organisés.
Après l'annonce, tout le monde fut soulagé.
Les élèves ont commencé à sortir de leurs

sièges, courant à la porte pour voir si le surintendant venait à leur classe.

Sit à votre place, dit Mme Jackson à sa classe.

Dès que les élèves se sont assis dans leurs sièges, a marché le surintendant.

WOW,
Quelle classe bien tenue.

Regardez ceci, tout le monde est dans leur SEAT!

NOW GUYS, voyez-vous l'importance de siéger à votre place, a demandé Mme Jackson.

Le surintendant a félicité la classe pour son succès et est parti pour continuer la visite de l'école.

# Sit In Your Seat Italian 530

I allarmi alla scuola elementare di Pamela suonavano in maniera incontrollata. Nessuno sapeva se si trattava di un falso allarme di una realtà minaccia.

Sit al suo posto, la signora Jackson gentilmente chiesto agli studenti in modo che potesse ascoltare per vedere se ci sarebbe stato un annuncio sopra l'altoparlante.

Hurry Up di classe, in fretta
 Ms. Jackson ha chiesto di nuovo.
Sedetevi al suo posto, fino a quando scopro
che cosa sta succedendo.


I studenti erano perplessi,
esecuzione per loro posti
contemporaneamente, con una sola
eccezione,
Tony.


Tony era uno studente di Ms. Jackson
amava, ma Tony ha avuto problemi di messa
a fuoco, che spesso hanno costretto la
signora Jackson di fermarsi e lui
reindirizzare nella classe.


Yes, la signora Jackson,
Tony ha risposto.

I bambini stavano parlando ad alta voce tra di loro, chiedendosi perché l'allarme era andare fuori.

Silence, essere in silenzio per un studenti minuti, la signora Jackson ha chiesto educatamente.
Ho bisogno di sentire l'annuncio.

Then è venuto,
L'annuncio.

I preside riceve l'altoparlante e ha annunciato l'arrivo del sovrintendente scolastico.

La principale ha voluto informare gli insegnanti che il sovrintendente stava facendo un giro della scuola per vedere che cosa tutto il vantarsi era circa.

It stato detto che 'studenti delle scuole elementari di Pamela ha segnato il più alto in lettura e matematica nel paese e sono stati anche classificati come più educato e organizzato.

12Dopo l'annuncio, ognuno è stato sollevato. Gli studenti hanno iniziato a uscire dalle loro sedi, correndo verso la porta per vedere se il sovrintendente era venuta alla loro classe.

Sit al suo posto, la signora Jackson ha detto alla sua classe.

Non appena gli studenti seduti ai loro posti, nel percorso il sovrintendente.

WOW,
ciò che una classe ben educati.

Guardate questo, tutti sono nella loro sede!

NOW RAGAZZI, vedi l'importanza di sedere al suo posto, ha chiesto alla signora Jackson.

Il sovrintendente si è congratulato con la classe sul loro successo e ha lasciato per continuare il giro della scuola.

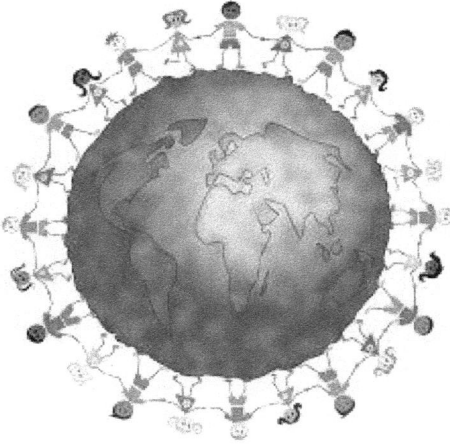

Special

Dedication To

## ALL THE CHILDREN WITH LOVE
## IN COUNTRIES AROUND
## THE WORLD

- A
- Afghanistan
- Albania
- Algeria
- Andorra
- Angola
- Antigua and Barbuda
- Argentina
- Armenia
- Australia
- Austria
- Azerbaijan
- B
- Bahamas
- Bahrain
- Bangladesh
- Barbados
- Belarus
- Belgium
- Belize
- Benin
- Bhutan

- Bolivia
- Bosnia and Hiszegovina
- Botswana
- Brazil
- Brunei
- Bulgaria
- Burkina Faso
- Burundi
- C
- Cabo Verde
- Cambodia
- Cameroon
- Canada
- Central African Republic (CAR)
- Chad
- Chile
- China
- Colombia
- Comoros
- Democratic Republic of the Congo
- Republic of the Congo
- Costa Rica
- Cote d'Ivoire
- Croatia
- Cuba
- Cyprus
- Czech Republic
- D
- Denmark
- Djibouti
- Dominica
- Dominican Republic
- E
- Ecuador
- Egypt
- El Salvador
- Equatorial Guinea
- Eritrea

- Estonia
- Ethiopia
- F
- Fiji
- Finland
- France
- G
- Gabon
- Gambia
- Georgia
- Germany
- Ghana
- Greece
- Grenada
- Guatemala
- Guinea
- Guinea-Bissau
- Guyana
- H
- Haiti
- Honduras
- Hungary
- I
- Iceland
- India
- Indonesia
- Iran
- Iraq
- Ireland
- Israel
- Italy
- J
- Jamaica
- Japan
- Shanna
- K
- Kazakhstan
- Kenya
- Kiribati
- Kosovo
- Kuwait
- Kyrgyzstan
- L
- Laos
- Latvia
- Lebanon
- Lesotho
- Liberia
- Libya
- Liechtenstein

- Lithuania
- Luxembourg
- M
- Macedonia
- Madagascar
- Malawi
- Malaysia
- Maldives
- Mali
- Malta
- Marshall Islands
- Mauritania
- Mauritius
- Mexico
- Micronesia
- Moldova
- Monaco
- Mongolia
- Montenegro
- Morocco
- Mozambique
- Myanmar (Burma)
- N
- Namibia
- Nauru
- Nepal
- Nethislands
- New Zealand
- Nicaragua
- Niger
- Nigeria
- North Korea
- Norway
- O
- Oman
- P
- Pakistan
- Palau
- Palestine
- Panama
- Papua New Guinea
- Paraguay
- Peru
- Philippines
- Poland
- Portugal
- Q

- Qatar
- R
- Romania
- Russia
- Rwanda
- S
- St. Kitts and Nevis
- St. Lucia
- St. Vincent and the Grenadines
- Samoa
- San Marino
- Sao Tome and Principe
- Saudi Arabia
- Senegal
- Serbia
- Seychelles
- Sierra Leone
- Singapore
- Slovakia
- Slovenia
- Solomon Islands
- Somalia
- South Africa
- South Korea
- South Sudan
- Spain
- Sri Lanka
- Sudan
- Suriname
- Swaziland
- Sweden
- Switzerland
- Syria
- T
- Taiwan
- Tajikistan
- Tanzania
- Thailand
- Timor-Leste
- Togo
- Tonga
- Trinidad and Tobago
- Tunisia

- Turkey
- Turkmenistan
- Tuvalu
- U
- Uganda
- Ukraine
- United Arab Emirates (UAE)
- United Kingdom (UK)
- United States of AmCarrynn (USA)
- 
- Uruguay
- Uzbekistan
- V
- Vanuatu
- Vatican City (Holy See)
- Venezuela
- Vietnam
- Y
- Yemen
- Z
- Zambia
- Zimbabwe

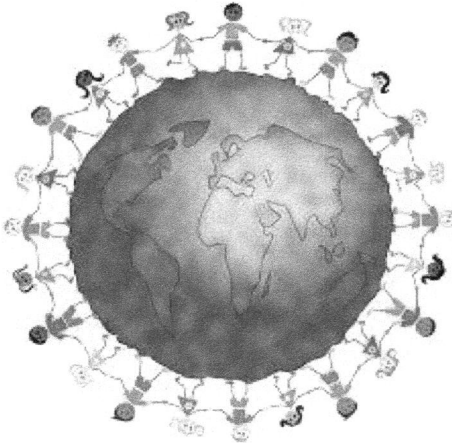

ANOTHER
SPECIAL DEDICATION TO ALL THE
CHILDREN WITH LOVE
IN CITIES IN THE
UNITED STATES OF AMERICA

Albany, NY
Albuquerque, NM
Anchorage, AK
Annapolis, MD
Atlanta, GA
Atlantic City, NJ
Augusta, ME
Austin, TX
Bakersfield, CA
Baltimore, MD
Baton Rouge, LA
Billings, MT

Biloxi, MS
Bismarck, ND
Bloomsburg, PA
Boise, ID
Boston, MA
Buffalo, NY
Burlington, VT
Carson City, NV
Charleston, SC
Charleston, WV
Charlotte, NC
Charlottesville, VA
Cheyenne, WY
Chicago, IL
Chicago, IL
Cleveland, OH
Colorado Springs, CO
Columbia, SC
Columbus, OH
Concord, CA
Concord, NH
Corpus Christi, TX
Dallas, TX
Davenport, IA
Daytona, FL

Denver, CO
Des Moines, IA
Des Plaines, IL
Detroit, MI
Dover, DE
Durham, NC
Erie, PA
Eugene, OR
Fayetteville, NC
Flagstaff, AZ
Frankfort, KY
Ft. Lauderdale, FL
Gettysburg, PA
Greenville, SC
Hampton Roads, VA
Harrisburg, PA
Hartford, CT
Helena, MT
Hollywood, CA
Honolulu, HI
Houston, TX
Huntsville, AL
Indianapolis, IN
Jackson, MS
Jackson Hole-Grand Tetons, WY

Jacksonville, FL
Jefferson City, MO
Jim Thorpe, PA
Juneau, AK
Kansas City, MO
Knoxville, TN
Lake Tahoe, NV
Lancaster, PA
Lancaster / Central PA
Lansing, MI
Las Vegas, NV
Las Vegas, NV
Lexington, KY
Lincoln, NE
Little Rock, AR
Long Island, NY
Los Angeles, CA
Los Angeles, CA
Louisville, KY
Madison, WI
Manchester, NH
Maryville, TN
Memphis, TN
Miami, FL
Miami, FL

Milwaukee, WI
Minneapolis, MN
Mobile, AL
Montgomery, AL
Montpelier, VT
Morrison, IL
Nashville, TN
New Haven, CT
New Orleans, LA
New York:  Bronx
New York:  Brooklyn
New York:  Manhattan
New York:  Queens
New York City
Newark, NJ
Niagara Falls, NY
Northville, MI
Oklahoma City, OK
Orlando, FL
Olympia, WA
Omaha, NE
Orange County, CA
Palm Springs, CA
Pensacola, FL
Philadelphia, PA

Phoenix, AZ
Pierre, SD
Pittsburgh, PA
Portland, ME
Portland, OR
Providence, RI
Pueblo, CO
Raleigh, NC
Rapid City, SD
Reno, NV
Richmond, VA
Sacramento, CA
Salt Lake City, UT
San Diego, CA
San Francisco, CA
Santa Cruz, CA
Santa Fe, NM
Scranton, PA
Seattle, WA
Sedona, AZ
Shreveport, LA
Silicon Valley, CA
Springfield, IL
St. Joseph, MO
St. Paul, MN

St. Louis, MO
State College, PA
SurfScranton, PA
Syracuse, NY
Tacoma, WA
Tallahassee, FL
Tampa, FL
Topeka, KS
Trenton, NJ
Tulsa, OK
Tuscon, AZ
Tyler, TX
Washington, DC
Wichita, KS
Wilkes-Barre, PA
Williamsburg, VA
Williamsport, PA
Wilmington, DE
Yuma, AZ

# Thank You

For Purchasing This Book
In Your Purchase, You Are
Celebrating With Me The
Completion Of One Of God's Many
Works Through Me.

## Pamela Denise Brown

# Contact Information
## Website:
Booksspeakforyou.com
1-800-757-0598
OR
267-318-8933
@Booksspeakforu (twitter)

## Email:
Booksspeakforyou@yahoo.com
FaceBook @Booksspeakforyou

BOOKS SPEAK FOR YOU

www.ingramcontent.com/pod-product-compliance
Lightning Source LLC
Chambersburg PA
CBHW071735020426
42331CB00008B/2037

* 9 7 8 1 6 4 0 5 0 1 6 1 4 *